EXTINGUISHED THINGS

by Molly Taylor

samuelfrench.co.uk

For Amateur Production Enquiries

United Kingdom and World
excluding north america
plays@samuelfrench.co.uk
020 7255 4302/01

Each title is subject to availability from Samuel French,
depending upon country of performance.

THINKING ABOUT PERFORMING A SHOW?

There are thousands of plays and musicals available to perform from Samuel French right now, and applying for a licence is easier and more affordable than you might think

---

From classic plays to brand new musicals, from monologues to epic dramas, there are shows for everyone.

Plays and musicals are protected by copyright law, so if you want to perform them, the first thing you'll need is a licence. This simple process helps support the playwright by ensuring they get paid for their work and means that you'll have the documents you need to stage the show in public.

Not all our shows are available to perform all the time, so it's important to check and apply for a licence before you start rehearsals or commit to doing the show.

LEARN MORE & FIND THOUSANDS OF SHOWS

Browse our full range of plays and musicals, and find out more about how to license a show

www.samuelfrench.co.uk/perform

Talk to the friendly experts in our Licensing team for advice on choosing a show and help with licensing

plays@samuelfrench.co.uk   020 7387 9373

Acting Editions

BORN TO PERFORM

Playscripts designed from the ground up to work the way you do in rehearsal, performance and study

---

Larger, clearer text for easier reading

Wider margins for notes

Performance features such as character and props lists, sound and lighting cues, and more

---

+ CHOOSE A SIZE AND STYLE TO SUIT YOU

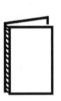

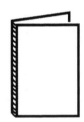

STANDARD EDITION

Our regular paperback book at our regular size

SPIRAL-BOUND EDITION

The same size as the Standard Edition, but with a sturdy, easy-to-fold, easy-to-hold spiral-bound spine

LARGE EDITION

A4 size and spiral bound, with larger text and a blank page for notes opposite every page of text – perfect for technical and directing use

LEARN MORE | samuelfrench.co.uk/actingeditions

MUSIC USE NOTE

Licensees are solely responsible for obtaining formal written permission from copyright owners to use copyrighted music in the performance of this play and are strongly cautioned to do so. If no such permission is obtained by the licensee, then the licensee must use only original music that the licensee owns and controls. Licensees are solely responsible and liable for all music clearances and shall indemnify the copyright owners of the play(s) and their licensing agent, Samuel French, against any costs, expenses, losses and liabilities arising from the use of music by licensees. Please contact the appropriate music licensing authority in your territory for the rights to any incidental music.

IMPORTANT BILLING AND CREDIT REQUIREMENTS

If you have obtained performance rights to this title, please refer to your licensing agreement for important billing and credit requirements.

ABOUT THE AUTHOR

Molly Taylor is a playwright and theatre-maker, based in London.

She began making work when she was an Associate of the National Theatre of Scotland. Her first production, *Love Letters to the Public Transport System*, toured Scotland in 2012 and won the Critics Circle Award, Adelaide Fringe 2018.

She works extensively in the participatory sector, making work with professional, and non-professional performers. She has made work for the Almeida, VAULT Festival, Young Vic, and Bush Theatre.

AUTHOR'S NOTE

The action is set in the present day and the past; it slips back in time to represent moments in Alton and Evie's lives, from the 2000s to the early 1970s. Music choices used to mark these transitions are up to the creative team.

The play is set within a single day – beginning briefly at Molly's childhood home in Liverpool before moving into Alton and Evie's house, down the road.

There are shifts in register; there is Molly in 'real time' in the house, Molly recalling her experiences there as a child, and the leaps back in time where we 'see' Alton and Evie in the home they created.

Alton and Evie's house can be represented by every single item referenced in the play – or none at all. The original production focused on a few select props to tell the story, and a backdrop of an epic net curtain, a very new carpet, and two standing lamps.

Molly is the narrator, and voices all the characters in the play. A dash in the text (-) indicates dialogue between two or more characters.

As much as possible the audience should be included in the play, Molly is telling this story to them, and should choose the moments when she wants to connect.

CREATIVE LIST

Molly Taylor - Writer and Performer

Molly Taylor is a playwright and theatre-maker who specialises in creating original performances inspired by the everyday.

Recent projects include: *Cacophony* (Almeida); *Shell and Davey at the Start and the End* (VAULT Festival); *And Yet It Moves* (Young Vic Taking Part); *See Me Now* (Young Vic/ HighTide/Look Left Look Right); *The Neighbourhood Project* (Bush Theatre) and *Love Letters to the Public Transport System* (National Theatre of Scotland).

Jade Lewis - Direction

Jade Lewis is a Theatre Maker and Director. Creative Associate at The Gate 2016 and a recipient of the Boris Karloff Award on Blackta (The Young Vic). She has facilitated for Company 3, Platform Islington, The Gate, The Bush Theatre, and directed.

Directing Ccedits include: *Extinguished Things* (Summerhall, Edinburgh); *Quarter Life Crisis* (Underbelly Cowgate and UK Tour); *On The Edge of Me* (Soho Theatre and UK Tour); *War and Peace* (Southwark Playhouse). Movement Director on *Followers* (Southwark Playhouse).

Assistant/Staff Director credits included: *Nine Night* (National Theatre and Trafalgar Studios); *A profoundly affectionate, passionate devotion to someone - Noun* (Royal Court); *The Convert* (The Gate); *Iphigenia Quartet* (The Gate) and *Venus/ Mars* (The Bush).

Naomi Kuyck-Cohen - Designer

Naomi Kuyck-Cohen is a theatre designer. Credits include: *Trap Street* (New Diorama); *And Yet It Moves* (Young Vic); *Nightclubbing* (The Lowry & Tour); *Passin' Thru* (Lyric Hammersmith); *Dreamplay* (The Vaults); *Trigger Warning* (Tate Modern); *In My Dreams I Dream I'm Dreaming* (Theatre Royal Plymouth); *I, Myself & Me* (Curve Theatre & UK Tour);

Rise: Macro vs. Micro (Old Vic New Voices); *FEAST* (Battersea Arts Centre).

Zak Macro - Lighting Design

Zak Macro is a lighting designer based in London. Having studied lighting design at The Royal Central School of Speech and Drama, Zak now works as a freelance designer and re-lighter for many venues and companies touring both nationally and internationally. His work spans Dance, Music, Theatre, and Opera.

Recent credits include: Lighting Design for *NOISE* (The Old Rep); *White Guy On The Bus* (Finborough); *Fenech-Soler* (OSLO Hackney); *The Weather Man* (Basic Space Festival); *We Can Make You Happy* (The Vaults); *Jenufa* (The ENO at Lilian Baylis); *Tomorrow* (Above the Arts Theatre) and *Death Of A Hunter* (Finborough).

Other credits include: Re-lighter and Technical Manager for *Chotto Desh* (Akram Khan and Sue Buckmaster World Tour) and Re-Lighter for *Until The Lions* (Akram Khan Company World Tour).

Miguel James - Sound Design

Aka Endlxssroll A Low-Fi hip-hop music producer and sound designer. Avid allotment keeper, bringing the awareness of healthy eating and affordable living, "grow your own beets".

Theatre credits include: *Quarter Life Crisis* by Yolanda Mercy.

Screen credits include: Project Diluted Aura (Film -title – TBC).

Music producing credits include: EndlxssRoll Beat tape – Rxxt_begin, Em-najidnal – Untitled Album (Italian).

Sound engineering credits: Fatal Assassins – Blue Borough Mixtap, Hungry Natsu Cooking, Eahwee – Healxng Sealings, Casio G-shock Sessions.

Sam Thornber - Production Manager

Sam Thornber has been working in the theatre industry for fifteen years. Studying at Edinburgh's Queen Margaret University and cutting his teeth as venue/stage Manager of the Udderbelly in the Edinburgh Fringe he then went on to work as Technical Stage Manager for companies including – National Theatre of Scotland, Stomp, Frantic Assembly, Sadlers Wells, Royal National Theatre, and others. He now spends most of his time working as a production carpenter for touring musicals.

Harriet Bolwell – Producer

Harriet Bolwell is a theatre producer. She is currently Assistant Producer at Paines Plough and Co-Founder & Co-Producer of *COMPLEX*. She was previously Producer at Produced Moon. Her credits include *Pop Music* (Paines Plough & Birmingham Repertory Theatre); *Roundabout Season 2018* (Paines Plough & Theatr Clwyd); *Taking Back Control* (COMPLEX.); *Seawall* (Paines Plough & The Old Vic); *I Wanna Be Yours* (Paines Plough & Tamasha); *Come To Where I'm From* (Paines Plough, Latitude Festival, The Tron, Hull Truck Theatre, Aberdeen Performing Arts & Marketing Gloucester); *Switchboard*, *in:humanity Eden Gate* and *The Hawke Papers* (Produced Moon).

ACKNOWLEDGMENTS

If it takes a village to raise a child, it takes countless people to make a one-woman show. Jade Lewis, who sat with me when it was just scraps of paper, timelines and questions and helped birth the show – thank you for your intelligence, sensitivity, and grace. To the Extinguished Things team for being a robustly charming crew and working your arses off – thank you for your commitment. Big thanks to Jonathan Hall, Charlie Taylor and Gary McNair for being trusted eyes, and serving up constructive advice when I needed it. To Linda and Dave Bacon, John and Deidre Gossage, Tricia and Owen Hagan, Alex Robinson and Perri Alleyne-Hughes, thanks for letting me into your homes to ask you about your lives (and look at your things). To my parents, for never asking me when I'm going to have a baby, or get a 'proper job' – you've put your weight behind my half-spun hopes for as long as I can remember. I'm truly really grateful for you both. But my greatest thanks go to Sam, who shouldered this show from its very inception, who bore the weight of it and me, and who, like Atlas, keeps everything aloft. You give me something to write about when I write about love. Thank you.

FIRST PERFORMANCE INFO

Extinguished Things was first performed at Anatomy Lecture Theatre, Summerhall at the Edinburgh Fringe Festival, on 1 August 2018.

The script went to press during rehearsals, and may differ from the text in performance.

CAST AND CREATIVE LIST

Written and performed by Molly Taylor

DIRECTOR   Jade Lewis
DESIGNER   Naomi Kuyck-Cohen
SOUND DESIGNER   Miguel James
LIGHTING DESIGNER   Zak Macro
PRODUCTION MANAGER   Sam Thornber
PRODUCER   Harriet Bolwell

CHARACTERS

MOLLY – A woman in her mid thirties

SETTING

The play takes place within a day, in two locations: in Molly's parents' house, and in the home of their neighbours, Alton and Evie, in Liverpool.

The world of the play has three registers: Molly in the present, Molly recalling past interactions with her neighbours, and the 'imagined' memories of Alton and Evie's lives together.

For Sue, Rogan, Charlie and Faith.
The best show on the road.

ACT ONE

Scene One: Being at home

In the space – a handful of domestic objects. A so-long-it's-epic net curtain. A fresh carpet. Two standing lamps. A table, with a drawer. Somewhere to make tea, a kettle, a mug, a sugar dispenser filled with tea bags. A bunch of vinyl records in a box.

MOLLY begins her story in the seating bank, speaks directly to the audience. She's taking them into her confidence, she's looking for an escape route.

MOLLY I'm back home, living with my parents again…yay! It's been a long time since I've lived here, seventeen years, but here I am…

Don't ask.

I'm in the kitchen. The cutlery drawer is a stainless steel horror show. Like the ladle and the fish slice have never stopped mating and producing offspring. It's the overflow drawer, where cutlery goes to die. In the left-hand corner, concealed under a pallete knife, are a set of keys.

These keys belong to a couple down the street, Al and Evie. They're away, on holiday, they must've been delayed, they haven't returned, no one has heard from them.

I don't know why we've got these keys, because God knows when we last used them. A decade. More. We've obviously forgotten to give them back, or they failed to ask.

Beat.

It wasn't a fight with my mum, it was terse words about the washing machine which I had overfilled because I couldn't see – with my own eyes – that they have a new model with a much smaller drum, and that overfilling it is a crime against engineering. So when it breaks – starts beeping and the door won't open, it isn't an argument it's just a breath-taking example of my lack of respect for this household.

I grab the keys. I can't resist. I just need a bolthole. I can check on the house. Give me mum some space. Just need a bit of fresh air, and then a bit of quiet. And if Alton and Evie are in, if they've returned, then I'll just – make up a reason why I'm knocking round. Sugar. Or something. And maybe they'll invite me in for a cup of tea. And I can hide.

Scene Two: Sevvy Park – Christmas – 2013

MOLLY *recalls.*

MOLLY Five years ago?

Christmas day. Or Boxing Day.

Sefton Park, which locals call Sevvy Park. On a map of Liverpool, it's a little kidney-shaped patch of green.

I'm walking it in, on my own. There's a couple coming towards me on the path. I can see their silhouette and I know their silhouette.

Evie, plumper than she used to be, swathed in layers, or scarves, I can't see where they start and where they end, she is like a willow tree. Al, tall and slimmer, still with a groove in his gait, dreadlocks peeping out from under his hat, bobbing as he walks.

I kind of groan inside, a disproportionate reaction. Sometimes you have those days when you can see the small-talk coming for you, slowly, like a drone. And you mentally pat your pockets for 'chat' – just anything, and you realise... No. I've got nothing.

I must've been tired, or hungover, and desperately enjoying my own company.

Evie clocks me and waves.

I haven't seen these two for a good few years, I don't come home as much as I should, and when I do there isn't a minute.

– Hello! How are you!

When close enough to touch I offer a hug, Evie first, which feels like the natural way to greet her, and then Al, which feels less natural, but we do it anyway.

– You're looking well – *you're* looking well – are you well?
– I am well, how are you? Very well – Merry Christmas!

They seem genuinely pleased to see me and I feel a pinch of guilt.

– How's your mum and dad? Is your dad still fishing? Are you still in London? Did you have your Indian takeaway for Christmas dinner? Did you???

Of course the answers to all these questions are yes, because we're still doing all the things we've always done, and this is good, because it's making them smile and it makes us seem more familiar.

They ask about my sisters; they want 'news'.

– Yeah they're both well.

I mean there genuinely isn't any news, no marriages, no babies, no house purchases.

– What are you up to?

– Just bits and bobs really. Nothing major.

They want to know about all of my life. I string something out.

Then – All power to your elbow! With a fist-pump from Evie.

Misplaced enthusiasm has a way of hollowing me out. I don't think I've got much more of this conversation in me. I feel very hungover.

– Well, keep in touch, we love to know what's going on.

– I will, I say – I will. Pause – Are you well?

I think that was the only thing I asked them during the whole conversation. Same question, three or four times.

– Yeah we're very well.

Evie looks up at Al as if to check in that that's the case, and he doesn't say anything but smirks, kisses her on her eyebrow. Nods at me.

– Keep on keeping on Molly.

Which feels like a good, clear sign-off.

That, to my memory, is the last time we spoke.

Scene Three: I Know This Place

MOLLY *on the move.*

MOLLY I walk down the road, towards number nineteen. I haven't lived on this road for a long time, but I know it well. I know the postbox at the end, on the corner, which doesn't actually accept post anymore because it's been decommissioned. I used to love running to that postbox, I used to fly to it, in that way that only children can, air-filled limbs full of lightness, like the wind kicking up. In my mind, that's how I used to run as a child.

I know the controversial purple wheelie bins, which Liverpool City council débuted at the end of the nineties.

– Well think about it! You can't have red bins, and you can't have blue bins. You've got to meet in the middle!

I know the church across the road, which I have never once attended, but I played hide and seek in the grounds.

I know the exact time of the day depending on how the sun hits the tarmac; the entire street a living sundial to me. I know this place like the back of my hand.

Scene Four: The Joy of Sex

MOLLY, *in Alton and Evie's house – strange yet familiar.*

MOLLY I ring the doorbell. No answer.

She handles the keys.

Do I?

I put the key in the lock.

Uninvited, I stand, in their narrow corridor. Looks normal – the same.

'Hello' – just checking.

There is a seven-inch vinyl record framed in their hallway, I remember it. It's been there so long now I know if it ever gets removed, there'll be a paler patch of wall beneath it, like a tan line.

I walk up the corridor, passing the entrance to the living room. A different sofa from last time, one of those L-shaped ones. Charcoal grey. I think it's really new. The carpet is possibly new too, it's quite spongey underfoot, in fact the whole room feels like it's been botoxed.

There's a photo on the mantelpiece, not framed, just propped up. Taken at a football match. Evie's eye caught mid-blink, and Alton's smile, broad, strong – a shoal of teeth.

The book shelf, on one side of the chimney breast, still there, and suddenly – I am thrust – for want of a better word – back to being a teen and discovering *The Joy of Sex*! Sitting on their bookshelf. Plain white cover, oh-so innocent, simple red text on the front. Astonishing to me that it was just sitting on the bookshelf, in the living room – in the middle of the *day*! Not a manual we had in my house. I can remember flicking through the pages, making watertight mental notes of exactly *where* it sat on the bookshelf – the paralysing FEAR that they would know that I had plucked it out and leafed through it. Line drawings of which I had never seen before – a man licking a woman's armpit, a hairy armpit. This was my awakening. No teen pornhub for my generation, no smart phone, or some shady video doing the rounds at school – it was a simpler time, people. You had to rely on your neighbours, to be out of the room long enough, for you to sneak a peek at a hand-drawn penis.

I'm back there, feasting on this book.

"Bathing together is a natural concomitant of sex and a splendid overture or tailpiece".

What the fuck?

"Taking an ordinary bath together has a charm of its own, although someone has to lean against the plumbing".

How right they were.

I want to find it; the white spine is easy to spot. No sign. Maybe it's in the bedroom where it's meant to be.

Beat.

My parents had prepared my sister's old room, which is luxuriated with a double bed, so they were a bit dismayed when I insist on sleeping in my old room, because the bed hasn't been changed, and there are boxes waiting to go to the charity shop, and it's a bit of a dumping ground.

But the heart wants what it wants, and I want my old room.

I'm sleeping in a single bed again. The simplicity of it.

MOLLY *places a bag, or a piece of clothing down in the space – she is staying. Pops the kettle on. Peaks into the drawer of the table, a bunch of letters live there. She handles them carefully, and begins to place them on the floor.*

There's a desk in the living room. A jigsaw of paper, stuck to the wall – postcards and quotes and handwritten statements. Prophets and philosophers; John Lennon, Allen Ginsberg.

A picture of a marbled face, a frowning Seneca. "We are not ill-supplied of life but we are wasteful of it".

When I see stuff like this it makes me want to be better at collecting.

There's a project underway. A pile of faded letters with two distinct sets of handwriting, dated 1942, 1943, 1944. In the folders, every yellowed letter has been transcribed.

Dear Terrence, Somehow I couldn't get around to writing yesterday eve. Still plugging along as usual. I cannot believe Christmas has come and gone.

Dear Rose, I will try to answer all of your questions. The first question you asked if I would be home by July, well I doubt that, in fact I'm sure that I won't, because it is already July. I believe that a tan is developing, not sure as yet but the red seems to be changing colour.

Evie's parents, I'm guessing, before her. Letters they had written, sent, kept and stored, and then married together. Left in the loft, for their daughter to find, after their death. Evie, in her retirement, must sit here, sift through them, type them out and fall backwards into her life.

Scene Five: What I've Left

MOLLY *goes to the freshly boiled kettle – adds one tea bag to a cup, then another, pours.*

MOLLY I only brought home what I could carry. I was quite limited. And I could feel Gav's silent judgement, because he's been telling me for years that I need to get a driving licence, or attempt at least a single lesson, and obviously I didn't. So when the time comes for me to depart, I can't even uphold my end of the bargain, which is to leave, cleanly. I go like a teenager, with a sulky backpack; I trust he'll know what to do after I've gone.

She drinks. Her fingers thumb through the letter rack. An order of service in her hands. She wants to piece this together – some of this is invention, some is based on prior knowledge. She is playing.

The night before Lol's funeral Al and Evie light a fire in their living room, in blatant disregard for the conventions of summer. It's a useless, damp June, and cloud lingers low in the sky in a sort of dense stupidity.

Al is looking over what he's written.

– Is it Doreen? His mum? Or Brenda?

Al isn't old, not old as we know it, but in his mid sixties where there were once names there are now tender gaps. Funerals aren't as rare as they used to be.

Two weeks earlier, they'd got the news of their friend. Evie prepping dinner, Alton coming in, he speaks with a different voice.

– It's Lol

Evie cries, briefly but steadily. Al speaks softly but matter-of-factly. It's a quiet stillness, this death, that mutes the room somehow. It manages to feels like something huge for a moment. Death is so strange, so jagged a concept.

Bewildering and painful and the most natural thing in the world. When Alton experiences it that day, it feels like fullness and nothingness in a perfect collision. Hard to get your head round.

Their friend Lol. Or Laurie. Who knew this couple, in the seventies. Before they knew each other. Back then, Alton had a mate Lol, who he'd gone to school with, and Evie had a friend Laurie, who she knew through going to clubs. And one night in the pub, when Alton taps her on the shoulder and says 'Meet Lol', Evie turns around to see her mate Laurie – they are one and the same. And everyone rejoiced. Lol was a link, which at the time felt like fate.

Now he's gone.

All the words they never bothered to attribute to him suddenly pop like bubbles.

– Lovely, decent, down-to-earth, kind, so kind, remember that time…

– Talented, decent, reliable.

– Proper, y'know, he was a *proper* person.

People always grow in stature in death.

Suddenly aware of the un-lived in space around her.

In Al and Evie's place there's a digital radio in every room. A turntable from a much cooler era. A CD player with proper speakers. A set of symbols on the top of the piano, and an electric keyboard in the spare room. Which looks like a music room, a mic on a stand.

But this place is so quiet.

No cats. Litter tray – gone. Feeding bowls, by the back door that opens out into the garden. Gone.

A discovery.

No life. We soon learn. The street learns. They are not coming home. A coach accident on holiday. Those nameless British tourists you hear about on the news bulletin.

Outside, the sun is bouncing on the tarmac, but in here – everything has ceased.

A moment to mark them.

ACT TWO

Scene Six: Tour of the House

MOLLY *with her tea, surveying the place – her past relationship to this house becoming real again.*

MOLLY I used to take the act of feeding the cats very seriously, because for those few days I was basically in charge of security. I thought my job was to uphold the fiction that Al and Evie were present in the house, like a game where I had to convince the whole street – call my bluff. So when I'd leave their house, I'd shout one-way conversations to the empty hallway.

– Thanks for the cookies Evie!

Always cookies.

I was playing at being a grown-up, because I was in charge of something, and that meant making up a story and playing it out.

I hated the cats. I could feel them mocking me when I fumbled with the tin opener. Nothing prepared me for the deeply meaty scent of spooned cat food. What on earth was this? Jellied chunky shit-flecked mulch.

We weren't a pet family. We believed in the absolute anonymity of goldfish.

There was one rule in Alton and Evie's house, that I couldn't let the cats out of the kitchen – they could get to the back garden through the cat flap in the back door, but they couldn't escape into the rest of the house. And they knew it. They just loved testing me. Waiting there at the kitchen door as I was due to leave, waiting for me to prise it open.

Once I had successfully escaped the kitchen I'd sometimes adjust the lighting in the hall and the upstairs landing. Which wasn't a rule but one I'd invented, to create another dimension to the 'fiction.'

For all I knew, everyone in the street knew that Al and Evie were away. But I must've been very aware of their house being vulnerable; we'd had countless burglaries in my house, throughout the eighties and nineties, snatched TVs and windows smashed, when I guess the city was really on the bones of its arse. So more than feeding the idiotic cats, I was guarding the place. In my mind. That's what they'd asked me to do.

Beat. **MOLLY** *is softer, a more internalised realisation.*

My parents want to know when I'm gonna know what I'm doing.

Which I suppose is fair enough.

But 'not knowing' is currently 'what I'm doing.' It's not a time-sensitive thing.

I don't know how long 'temporarily' is – but in my mind it means 'not forever'. So can we go with that. I am here, back home, for 'not forever.' If that's ok.

– You can stay here as long as you need to.

Which is great.

But.

There is an expectation that being here is the start of the end of the not knowing.

Scene Seven: New Year's Eve countdown, 1998 – Almost 1999

The house suddenly alive – a party. Muffled Marvin Gaye*. The hustle of giddy drinking. The most populated their house ever was. MOLLY *takes it in.*

MOLLY Alton and Evie are hosting. On the cusp of a new year, on the cusp of fifty, twenty-odd years of marriage behind them.

Boxes of wine are being tipped and squeezed, to deliver every last drop. In some cases the aluminium bags of wine within have been wrenched free, so it looks like a space-age drinks party.

This was a hastily organised event. You could call it a diversion. This couple have masterminded the best way to ignore the passage of time, and that's to celebrate it. What better than a house full of people wedging themselves perfectly between them? They will barely need to speak

Ten – Alton is looking at his watch, it's two minutes slow, he's checking it against someone else's – hang on a minute. They don't want multiple countdowns.

Nine – Evie is opening the door to the back garden, she's shocked to find an inch of snow has fallen in the last hour.

Eight – Doorbell rings, Alton answers. He knows one face out of the four, a perfect ratio – You're cutting it fine!

Seven – Evie is evacuating cava from a bottle, filling up grateful glasses.

Six – A glass is nudged off the table and smashes on the floor.

Five – The countdown is in danger of being lost to confusion. The telly in the living room is switched on, Big Ben,

---

* A licence to produce EXTINGUISHED THINGS does not include a performance licence for music by Marvin Gaye. For further information, please see Music Use Note on page v.

an irrelevant monument at every other time of the year, becomes the focal point.

Four – Alton hovers in the living room. Evie hides in the kitchen, they will each host their way through midnight, they'll keep filling glasses, they won't kiss.

Three – Where's your coal bucket? Someone is insisting on bringing a piece of coal into the house, for first footfall, after midnight. Back door open again. Evie directs them. The snow is fresh, within seconds they have slipped and fallen onto their hands and knees.

Two – Someone else is in the garden, drawn like a child to the fresh snow, and lies down, arms and legs splayed to make a snow angel.

One – The room takes a breath...

The bells.

HAPPY NEW YEAR! Like a goal has been scored, it's January again. Alton pours a drop of rum onto the front step. Party pops. The coal is brought, staggering into the house. Wine swills. Goodwill swells. Someone bravely attempts Auld Lang Syne. Evie is looking at the snowfall in the garden, and the two shapes imprinted on the lawn; one you can tell is an angel, but the other is just a mess of trampled snow.

Scene Eight: Handing the Keys Back

MOLLY *with Evie's letters, sorting them – aimlessly.*
Something raw and a bit hard about her – almost a
confession wedged in her throat. She fights it: tears,
failure, whatever it is.

MOLLY I was meant to wait for him. Gav. To give him the keys
back, which I didn't think was necessary, but he wanted a
moment, I think, or something final, an image in his head
of the end. Some gutting goodbye. I think it's dangerous to
have an idea in your head of what these moments should
look like and sound like, because they are based on false,
filmic stories and endings, and if we'd all been brought up
with purely documentary evidence then we'd never ever
stage manage a goodbye in our lives, because it would be
so underwhelming, so easy and pathetic, that we couldn't
bear the idea that life's pain is so prosaic. We'd never ever
say goodbye. Which isn't the same as staying together.

He sent me a text.

– I'm on the bus, it's changing over driver, but the new
driver isn't here yet. Wait for me.

But I had a train to catch, and he knows I like to be at the
station with plenty of time.

So I pulled the door to, and posted the keys through the
letterbox.

And I cried all the way to the station. And people are quite
good in London, you can cry in public quite openly and
no one bothers you much. But on the tube a woman leant
forward and asked "Are you ok?"

And I couldn't answer.

Scene Nine: Locked Out

To her mug of tea – a distraction.

MOLLY I remember being here as a child. An after-school cock-up. Someone was dropping me home, but there was no one in. Al and Evie's was the first door that opened.

Al had a bowl of cereal in his hand when he opened the door – which was just so wacky to me. To be eating breakfast in the afternoon. Like he'd failed this really simple task.

– Yeah, yeah, yeah, come in, yeah, sure I can keep an eye on her.

I hadn't been in their house before, but I'd knocked at their door at Halloween, and I knew them because we were always playing out – we used to sit in my dad's parked car, for hours, playing Back to the Future – going nowhere slowly – and we'd see them walking past and beep at them and they'd wave. So I knew who they were.

But because they didn't have kids, I'd never been in their house before.

I sat down at the table, which seemed huge, and Alton was asking about my day at school, and I was awkward and instantly homesick, six doors down. I was painfully shy and I couldn't believe that he wasn't. We didn't belong sitting round this table together.

At one point he sat me down at the piano which was a relief, and we probably burnt a solid hour there, teaching me a simple tune. I remember that whilst I was there he was pretty much hanging out with me the whole time. He didn't put me in front of the telly and get on with something more important.

Because it got late, and we still hadn't sourced a parent, Al suggested we eat – a bowl of pasta – which was a comfort. He had a tea towel over his arm, like a waiter. This little flourish when he handed me the bowl. Wholemeal pasta. So foreign to me. Devastating.

I didn't eat it. I told him I had a stomach ache and didn't feel well. I remember his concern. Standing there with the fridge door open, backlit by the glow, looking for something else to offer me.

– We weren't expecting guests Molly.

Scene Ten: Bathroom – 1989

MOLLY *is in the bathroom, a dripping tap.*

MOLLY Evie wipes the snot away from her face with her hand. Plunges it in the bath water.

She's sitting upright, it's dark, the bulb in the bathroom has gone and they don't have one to replace it. It's one of those days. The door is propped open so the light from the hall can filter in half-heartedly, a meek creamy light that makes the tiles look jaundiced, as if this is a room built for sickness, but Evie knows that she is not sick.

Alton is crouching next to her, clothed and dry. She knows he's there but she doesn't look up.

– It'll happen. It will.

– I know it will, will you stop fucking saying that.

Words are pallid, so he reaches out and grabs her hand and this, she accepts.

They sit there like this for minutes, the side of the bath a border between them – the land and the sea. Different continents.

Alton wants to get in the bath. He should get in the bath. He's going to, he's going to do it. He'll just slip in, there – in that space, it'll be a bit awkward, a bit clumsy, Evie will, momentarily have his penis quite close to her face, and he won't be able to sit down, but he could kneel, kneel next to her, maybe. If that isn't, if that's, is that helpful, no – he's not going to do it, there's not enough room, he doesn't want to disrupt. Give her some space.

If he knew what to sing, he'd sing her something.

He catches her eye and tries to smile. She tries to return it.

Alton's experience of this particular pain, at this particular moment, manages to be doubled and diluted. The doubling is watching his wife's grief, multiplying his own, and the dilution because it's all happening outside of him. She is the sole focus of his care, and he cannot do anything for her. What great trickery of manhood, that the scale of his incompetency has been concealed from him until now.

– Cold.

– Course yep.

He turns the hot tap on, a hard gush.

– Warm you up now.

It runs and runs. Evie shrinks.

– Cold – she says again.

– Ah fuck.

No hot water.

– Sorry love.

Why hadn't he just gone with a trickle to check?

– I'll do a kettle.

He's up, he's off.

It's dark and quiet and cold and horrible in here.

Evie lets out a curdling fart in the bath, it warms her briefly.

A few feet away the kettle boils. Alton thinks – drink. Rum. Whisky. What have they got? Finds a glass. Pour. Kettle shuddering. Steam. He looks for a mug. But he's not making tea! Picks up the brandy in one hand, the kettle in another.

– Here, have this.

Glass is in her hand, the smell. She looks at him incredulous.

– I'm not drinking – she almost says.

– Watch yourself.

The kettle arcs. Evie shrinks again.

– That better?

It's now ferociously boiling where her feet should be, and freezing where her arse is. Alton swills the water around

– Better?

Barely. He fills it from the bath tap and into the kitchen again. Switch. Boil. Shudder. He wishes he had the brandy.

Evie gripping the glass. Not drinking, hasn't been. But now, she can. Doesn't want to.

Another kettle in. Instantly scalding, then briefly perfect, then cooled again. How many fucking kettles is it going to take? Alton's taken it on like a race. Neither suggests that she should get out of the bath.

Third kettle in. Almost like a relief. It's dark and quiet and slightly less cold in here but it's still horrible.

– Is that better?

– I don't want this.

Glass outstretched.

– I don't want this.

And she's crying. With the kettle poised over the cold bath in the near-dark, never more pathetic than this. The hapless, hopeless attempts to correct the incorrectible. Never has she hated Alton more for trying to make something, anything OK. It's grim, like all the light in the world is fading, and it's cracking her insides open.

And Alton is in the bath, he's there, fully clothed and crouching and trying to fold himself into her, sodden socks slipping, trying to hoist her up and get down to where she is, begging for contact or to take some weight.

– Come here, come here.

He clutches her, she lets him, they hold each other in the cooling pool of bathwater.

– I know, I know he says – I know.

But he also recognises, in the same breath that he doesn't.

Beat. **MOLLY** *observes this moment; it sits with her.*

Around the dinner table, six doors up, four nights ago. I've drunk wine before dinner. Error. My parents are x-raying me with concerned eyes, as the conversation tiptoes around the question of my gene pool – their gene pool. The future of that gene pool. A subtle attack on a single woman; an elephant in the womb.

– Because I don't want... I don't want...

– You don't want what?

– I don't want to waste my youth!

Mum hoots.

– Your youth?

At thirty five she thinks I clearly have no chance of 'wasting my youth'. Because I've done that already.

– No, but, I mean, I want to be able to make the *most* of my...freedom – yeah – fuck it – my youth!

– Don't speak with your mouth full.

She twirls some spaghetti around her fork.

– Do you remember when I told you about periods Moll?

I'm dying to see how this is relevant.

– And you cried.

– Periods are scary when you're twelve.

My dad has picked up his plate and gone into the kitchen.

– And I said 'There's nothing to be scared of, every woman goes through this'.

– Yeah.

– And you said 'Why does it have to change?'

To me, that seems like a perfectly good question. The burden of biology.

– Can I just eat my dinner?

Scene Eleven: The Riots – 1981

Amidst the selection of vinyl records, **MOLLY** *selects an LP.*

MOLLY It's July 1981. Six doors up, my mum is breathing hard, I'm about to be born.

Evie is twenty-eight, Alton twenty-nine. Married for four years. And this song – *Ghost Town,* by the Specials** – will be Number 1 on the Hit Parade on Sunday.

A few streets away in Toxteth a war has broken out on the streets. It's not unfamiliar – the Brixton Riots that April, the St Pauls riots in Bristol the previous year.

But on this week in 1981, somewhere between Tuesday and Thursday Evie loses her mind.

She hasn't seen Alton for two nights, since he headed out to meet Lol.

– Don't forget to take the saxophone, will you?

– Not tonight, I'll drop it off to him maybe next week.

– Drop it off tonight.

– I promise I will do it.

– Alton.

This conversation needs a full stop because they have had it a dozen times.

– Look, I can't open the door.

Evie is gesturing in the narrow hallway to their flat where the saxophone case currently lives, propped up against the wall, and, like clockwork, when the door opens the saxophone case slides down onto the floor and blocks her entry.

** A licence to produce EXTINGUISHED THINGS does not include a performance licence for GHOST TOWN by THE SPECIALS. For further information, please see Music Use Note on page v.

– I know, I know, I know – he says – but if I just move it to the bedroom.

– Or...you could just do what you said you were gonna do a month ago.

This is the end of the conversation, Evie walks away. She hears the front door swing shut. An hour later, she goes out into the hallway and the saxophone case is gone.

Two nights later Alton still hasn't come home and the saxophone case is lodged like a splinter in her mind. It belongs to Lol, but he left it here weeks ago in protest – he's been stopped and searched by the police eight times whilst carrying his saxophone to and from gigs. Young black men like him can't expect anything else in this city right now. Alton has resisted carrying that case around him for exactly the same reason, too much fucking hassle. Evie stupidly, naively thinks that there's bound to be a night's grace, there's bound to be a night when Alton can walk down the street, immune from the police. But he's not here to prove that. And what's more, she encouraged Lol to leave that saxophone here in the first place, because she agreed it was safer than carrying it home, and it takes weeks, a few brief weeks for her to forget that and prioritise the available space in her hallway. Her care is fraudulent.

And outside buildings are starting to burn.

Race riots. That's what they are being called. And Evie can't believe that. She can't believe that factions of her city, the white community that she belongs to, and the black community that Alton belongs to, are at war.

Beat.

Hours later. Knock at the door. Alton?

No. Mike and Dave, two brothers, Jewish lads, friends of theirs.

– Can't get up Upper Parliament street. Barricaded it. Can't get through town. Fucking crazy out there. Had to turn back. Can't get through.

– You OK?

– You OK?

– You OK?

Everyone checks. No one has seen Alton.

– He'll be at his mum's. If he's at his mum's he won't be able to get out, they've blocked it off.

– The Rialto is on fire. Whole place just gone up.

Evie is grabbing her bag.

– No, no, no, no – Evie. Seriously.

Evie's fear is like cement.

– No, no they're not fighting each other Evie! It's not like a race thing, they're fighting the police. It's the coppers, it's the fucking coppers they're after!

– Look, he'll be fine, he'll be fine. He's not daft. Look. Come here.

The city's senses are overwhelmed. Smashed glass and hurled bricks. The smell of lit petrol. But in Evie and Alton's flat everything looks just so peachy normal. No chaos, here.

Cups of tea become brandy, and the brandy cuts through the quiet in the flat, Mike and Dave, going nowhere tonight, keep watch with Evie, and through heated speech take the city apart. The place is fucked. Jobs are a memory. People are skint. Punitive police, racist police. Crackdowns. Club closures. Stop and search. Tough luck. The conversation gets heated, as if the combined energy of their words can somehow fuel the uprising beyond the doors. A city on its knees and a fight on its hands. This isn't new, none of it is new, but tonight it's news.

It's one am and two am and three am, and soon the sun will be up, and Evie will be really, really grateful for that sun, deterred by nothing. What a thing, to be able to rely on the dawn. She places her faith in daylight, as if it can bring with it a solution. She's a bit pissed.

Evie has dropped off. Front door opens. Her eyes too. Where is she? Couch. Door closes. Blinks. Alton. He's in the hallway, rigid as a tree, a gash on his forehead, above his left eye. And Evie is just hugging him. He doesn't reciprocate. She's holding him, holding him, holding him to make sure he's real, and when she pulls away she notices he's weeping and in the years they've been together she's never seen him weep before.

Later, Alton wants to walk. When it all dies down he wants to walk up the road. It shouldn't seem so radical, this. The place looks monochrome, colour bleached by fire. Paving stones have been liberated. It's quiet.

There is a duckling, in the middle of the road. It doesn't fly away as they approach it. It looks like it's been drafted in by the park department to prove something. Alton bends down to pick it up, it weaves out of his hands, so that Evie has to take off her cardigan and gather it up. They look at it.

– What are we going to do with it?

They walk to the lake in Princes Park. It's a relief to see water.

Scene Twelve: Me and the City

MOLLY *observing the space where Alton and Evie have just stood. She's working something out.*

I've lived away almost longer than I lived here, but when I'm asked, I'm never from anywhere else. I still claim this city.

But in truth, I don't ever commit. I wait until I feel accepted by a place and then I know can leave.

I don't carry its scars. I can't imagine what it takes to stay.

I've retreated back here, but I'm an interloper. Even in my birth town, now, people want to know where I am from.

I want to be definite about something.

Suddenly – a memory pops, she grabs her tea. Something makes sense.

It must have been a geography project, at some point in my teens I come round here to interview the couple. 'Comparing and contrasting three areas of Liverpool'; I'm collecting data for my graphs.

I'm happy to stand on the doorstep and fire questions from there, but Evie won't have it, come in, come in, come in.

She shouts out to Alton.

– Molly is doing a project Alton can you give us five minutes?

We are in the living room, and sitting on the couch – the old one – feels weirdly formal, a stilted chat show. These are doorstep questions. When Alton swings through the door he's got a steaming cup of herbal tea. He's a double-bagger. Two tea bags in the same mug.

I'm looking at my questionnaire, first question.

– Where are you from?

– I'm from Clitheroe.

Straightforward answer from Evie, but I can't spell it.

– Ermmm, well I was born here Moll, I'm from here but me ma is Irish and me dad's from, my dad was Jamaican.

I've only got a small box and I don't know what to write down.

– Here y'are, put 'From the sea'.

Beat.

Not me now, someone else, a different teenager, a lad. Carlos. Who sent the thank you card stuck to the fridge.

'Yous have been so good to me over the last few months, big thanks for taking me in like that, I owe yous'.

Carlos is seventeen years old, a short lad, crop of thick black hair and he leans on *everything*, it doesn't matter where he is, he finds a surface to support him. So when he's in the kitchen with them, leaning on the worktop they constantly have to buffer him from one section to another, as they try and make dinner, slows everything in the kitchen down.

The vintage Tate and Lyle sugar dispenser – Alton is weaving a story around it.

– We were at the Albert dock the other day weren't we, and we walked past the Tate.

He pulls the sugar dispenser into position.

– Sitting in this ripe position in the dock, the great mouth of Britain at one point, and I'm thinking this is where the ships all came in, trade that was built off the slaves, and here we are at the Tate, a cultural totem built out of the sugar.

– That was my mother's – Evie tells Carlos, who is less interested in the dispenser.

– Yeah, yeah, yeah, yeah, yeah – Carlos ditched history gladly at fourteen, but he's totally plugged in to what Alton is saying at this moment.

Evie's half-listening. There are soggy scraps of yesterday's dinner in the plughole. Carlos doesn't practice the art of emptying his plate before he rinses it with water. Every day, a different selection of wet shreds.

They aren't used to having a teenager in the house. Every morning, an extra face to greet. The imbalance of the bathroom door being locked and both she and Alton forming a queue.

It's been lovely, and strange.

There are people in Evie's life who look at the simple form of her marriage, the clean symmetry of it – and envy her. No ruptures from child-rearing. They hold up her holiday destinations as her prize.

It's innocently thoughtless, this assumption. Evie knows, but isn't often asked, about what it feels like; the soft low daily hum of being an un-mother. The sensation doesn't recede after forty-five, fifty or fifty-five. It doesn't retire. It is definitive. A lifelong project. Her friends' children have children. Evie sends babygrows and hungry caterpillars, she knows the checklist. And she genuinely cares. And it genuinely matters. And it genuinely never stopped mattering for her.

Alton's conversation has ricocheted on. They are getting louder.

- Can I just get to the – Evie needs to get under the sink.

Carlos ambles away, stands against the cooker, *leans* so hard she can hear the tick tick tick tick of the igniter. He rearranges himself. But now she needs to get to the cooker.

Evie is genuinely happy to host him. But the toast crumbs in the butter. She can't believe how taxing it all is.

Alton is in full voice.

Maybe she'll ask them to go into the living room.

He is talking about the poisonous graffiti of his youth – 'klu klux clan'.

– Clan spelt with a C, like. Fucking dickheads.

Grim amusement.

– I remember getting set on by some white skinheads, walking through the park, they'd been fishing. Bamboo fishing rods, and they attacked us, me and Lol, we were only about nine or ten, and they whipped us with these home-made fishing rods. Literally my back getting whipped.

Evie is looking at her husband, as he levels with Carlos – the sheer shock of the child in him, grown into a parent, bestowing painful wisdom onto the shoulders of a young boy. He's not looking at her. He's watching his friend. She is looking at his profile. She is quiet, she is listening. He is speaking. Carlos is leaning in.

And when Alton gets to the end of this chapter it's silent briefly.

– You never told me that – she says – I never knew that.

He turns to her, extends his arm out, and beckons her towards him.

ACT THREE

Scene Thirteen: The Kop

MOLLY *finds an old football scarf, red and white striped,*
unbranded – innocent. Something charged about it.

MOLLY Alton is walking through the front door, with Evie on
his back, she's got no shoes on, but this scarf round her
neck. Her soles are soot-black, filthy, Alton is trying to put
her down at the foot of the stairs.

– No no no kitchen!

Placed on a worktop next to the sink Evie is kicking her
feet up.

– Look at the fucking state of them.

Alton grabs her left foot, brings it up to his mouth as if to
kiss it – No!

– I might have rabies.

There's water filling the sink, and Evie is giddy and dirty
and ecstatic. Holding on to the scarf like a life jacket.

– We're going back next week – a statement, not a question
from Evie.

– We're away next week.

– Are we? She thinks he means them, but he means the team.

– Look – he levels with her – I think they're gone.

Feet plunged into water.

– I can't, I can't – she can't believe it, she can't believe it.

Hours earlier, she was ordained, christened in the full spit and fury of the Kop, introduced by this man who now, in 1975, is living with her, in the fullness of sin.

On top of the record box.

Alton has plugged her into this energy source known as Anfield, a place of thunder and light, and she was *light* on those feet of hers, lifted, shoulder-to-shoulder with thirty thousand others. The force of it. She can't believe it. A goal, another, another, another, five in total, Ipswich Town obliterated, and the crowd surging forward, with her, she cannot give consent, she cannot argue, she's in the sea. Alton is the raft.

Thrilling, thrilling and stupid. Her feet are off the floor, she is airborne for moments, her clogs, leather-bound and wooden soled, so foolishly selected that morning slipping off, her toes scrunching up – stay with me clogs! The crowd lurches forward again and her clogs are gone, they're gone, like an offering to the gods, these gods on the pitch, she has sacrificed her shoes! And she is flying!

Alton knows Evie has never belonged to this city before, in the four years since she moved here, but today, he put her marker down, today he indoctrinated her into the mythic. Liverpool didn't win the league that year, but that day Evie lost her clogs on the Kop, which was more important, and Alton knows he has gifted her this most delicious of birthdays, a lit flame behind her eyes, and in the foolish exhilaration of it all, he has inextricably made her into an 'us'.

– Come on cinders.

He held out a towel.

MOLLY *glances at the space where their photo resides, on the mantelpiece. She connects.*

Passed like a baton from Alton to Evie. He gave her something that can't be taught, and she kept it with her for life.

I don't know who gets to keep this now – this token, or if it just belongs here. Who does it get passed down to now?

Beat.

Maybe sometimes you receive and you only give so much.

He indoctrinated her into the mythic.

The space, unveiling itself. During this section **MOLLY** *slowly begins to re-set the space, carefully placing back every item she has moved or handled, suddenly aware of the delicacy of these relics.*

She stuck the gig tickets around the mirror.

He framed the record.

She picked the paint.

He carried her mother's letters down from the loft.

She collected his medication.

In the bathroom, the prescription bottles with tiny typeface.

On the side, the plant spray for the spider plants, and their little spider babies.

The orders of service, that slowly multiply.

The greyly faded velvet wedding dress that Evie's mother refused to come and bear witness to.

The towels they bickered about in the John Lewis sale, or the Home and Bargain sale, or the Linen Warehouse sale.

Their handwriting, on notes, and cards, and crosswords and calendars, wallpapering their lives with fleeting words.

In the bedroom. Matched socks, not a stray amongst them.

Functional bras.

Patterned tights bundled up together, an octopus of empty legs.

These curious fossils.

On the bedside table, a book, with a bookmark, forever suspended in the middle of it.

The bed.

All of this.

The cathedral of it.

The people of no significance, becoming holy.

Go back.

Did they still touch each other's skin, slackened and mottled, and scarred, and already dying – from the daily dying of just living? Did they? Are they touching each other now?

Going back.

These tiny testaments, soon to be stripped, soon to disappear, but for this moment preserving their shape, their imperfect outline.

Going back.

And back, and back and back.

Scene Fourteen: Early Days

MOLLY *perches on the table, cup of tea in hand, she has a front-row seat, she can see this young couple in the space.*

MOLLY They have made this flat a fortress, overnight. No one has stepped over the threshold since they got home on Friday, and no one does, until the following Tuesday. It's hard for either of them to know who started it.

They are silently egging each other on to resist the spinning of the earth, who is going to come out victorious – these two fresh lovers or the dulling ubiquity of *time*. Time never does anything *new*. And new is all they are to each other.

These four days have two gears; the first is an easy orbit, where they float in the same space around each other, and the second is when they are together, and burning. Alton and Evie are no strangers to sex. But when their limbs bend and blend with each other's, it is made strange. Their eyes are always open, startling in its bravery, an admission of something they don't understand. The most important thing you never learn to say. For this brief window of time, they have never been more of their bodies.

They are young, so young, and at nineteen and twenty, older than they have ever been.

Alton isn't aware of the striking beauty that he possesses, He thinks not of his hipbones and shoulder blades, the sharp angles he can cut. He is so cavalier, so un-moved by these physical gifts. He is just a man, or he is becoming a man, and he takes for granted that every inch of him is doing something spectacular, all of the time.

For Evie, being under Alton's gaze is intoxicating, she is clumsily drunk on having an audience, and it's altering everything about the space. Never before has she expended so much energy on how to stand, how to frame her body in new and intriguing ways. Alton doesn't notice this performance. He's just watching *her*.

Day three and they are on rations. Occasionally Alton makes a polite attempt to find his clothes. Evie is on the cusp of giddy.

– I think on the back of the settee with your waistcoast. Waistcoast. Is that right? What's wrong with a waistcoast? Alton, why can't I say waistcoast??? Alton. Waiscoast! Argh.

They need more oxygen.

It's day four, Monday, and Evie knows that her pint of milk is on the front step, and she's convinced that if she opens the door to collect it, Alton will wake up to the world that lies beyond it and he'll leave. And if he leaves, she knows she won't see him again.

Alton is wondering when he's going to get kicked out. Hospitality like this is rare. He clears his throat. It's a Monday. Does he need to pretend he has somewhere to be?

It's amazing what a body can do when it won't speak.

And these are the days before things are spoken, before words and phrases are massaged into white noise, before those times when you speak and don't listen, when you hear but don't tell. This is before you claim to know what you want. Before you claim to know anything. This is the wonderful not-knowing.

His hand is on her neck.

Her fingers on his ribcage.

The flesh of her shoulder in his mouth.

Teeth.

Ouch!

Apology.

Laughter.

Hips release.

Nerves in flight.

Brains lit up.

For no one to see.

Before the need for clarity.

Before the need to work out where you're going.

Before you make a sacrifice.

Before you learn to overlook it.

Before you replay it in your head.

Before you hold it up as an example.

Before you know regret.

Before you forget.

Before you.

Before you.

It's all before you.

Later, when it's quiet. Alton's face rests in her neck, his mouth casual on her skin. He is still. Under his lips, he can feel her pulse. A drum beat of blood flickering against his skin – now, and now, and now, as if to reach up and remind him.

Daylight. They lie and look at each other. Evie feels a hand play a scale down her back, all the way down, each vertebrae a semitone, until Alton's hand rests on her hipbone. He grips it. It was made to fit into his palm. A lightning smile.

– You have a lovely skeleton.

And it is maybe this, for Evie. The sensation of this. Of all the facile compliments she will gather in her lifetime, the easy assessments of her smile, her eyes, this is a phrase she will only ever hear once. If it's possible for words to change physiology, then it happens now. It takes root. This sensation, of someone simply loving the bones of her.

Beat.

I'm in the living room.

I'm looking at that photo of them on the mantelpiece and they are beaming back at me.

It's a. Living. Room.

In the grate of the fire, ashes and ashes and dust and dust, from the last time Evie lit the fire, or Alton lit the fire, whoever's creaking knees took on that task, which they did for the last time without knowing.

And in the coal bucket there's six pieces of coal. The largest one is as big as my fist, and the smallest one the size of a new potato. I think it might be the oldest thing I've ever seen. Their coal bucket hosts millions of years of something. Of matter. Living matter, once. Heat and pressure and years ago. I cannot even begin to explain how it got here, because I don't know.

All the things I'll never know about this place. Summed up strangely in six pieces of coal.

Coming through the door on New Year's Eve.

Spotlighting their faces. Through decades.

These six pieces not burnt that night. Bed, early to bed, or gone out – the fire, too late, or forgotten, or no need to waste it, because the day is over. The climb of the stairs, the bannister, always there, still there, the light switch in the hallway, mucky with finger tips, always there, still there. The worn carpet at the foot of the bedroom door, still there, the curtains to pull, the barrier to the light of the sun, every day, always there. The duvet, sometimes clean, always there. The pillow that knows you well, too well, that's there, still there, with the microscopic parts of you that you left behind, the skin you were living in, until that moment, when you lay down, and you rolled over and you left a trace of yourself there.

Maybe these six pieces of coal will never be burnt now. They have reached some sort of ending, in the room of Alton and Evie's living.

I am not far behind them. In the grand scheme of things, none of us are that far behind them. We know, and *don't* know where we are going – 'after'. It's all unknown. So all we ever have is *this*. All they had is *this*, for as long as they existed, which – however you look at it – was for the tiniest fraction of time.

We only have all of this.

Life is not short, but we make it so.

I have this.

I want to move, I want to leave, I want to stay, I want to say goodbye.

I pull the front door to. I post the keys through the letterbox.

And I run.

I run towards the postbox at the end of the road.

The bobbing, jerking horizon, my tumbling running legs, the ground tread-milling beneath me. I run as if I might take off. I am in flight. I am awake. A towering feeling of being alive. The most wasted sensation in the world.

I run to the postbox that doesn't accept post, as useless and valuable as it is. Just like life, just like life.

I run.

End

PROPS
(from original production, but open to interpretation)

Table with a drawer
Kettle
Mug tree and mugs
A vintage Tate and Lyle sugar dispenser
Tea bags (kept in sugar dispenser)
A letter rack with bills, letters, envelopes
An order of service for Laurence Johnson's funeral
A box full of vinyl records (that can be sat on)
Letters from WWII, plus typed-up transcriptions
A set of keys

SOUND EFFECTS

SCENE 5: A coal fire under Lol's funeral section
SCENE 7: New Year's Eve – muffled music from the party in the background
SCENE 10: Bathroom – a water dripping effect
SCENE 11: Riots – *Ghost Town* by The Specials or a riot soundscape
SCENE 12: Kitchen soundscape under the Carlos section
SCENE 13: The Kop – a football crowd in the background

THIS
IS
NOT
THE
END